THE EVERGLADES

Tamra B. Orr

Kids' Guide to History, Wildlife, Plant Life, and Preservation

Paperback ISBN 979-8-89094-066-7
Hardcover ISBN 979-8-89094-067-4

The Cataloging-in-Publication Data in on file with the Library of Congress.

To learn more about the other great books from Fox Chapel Publishing, or to find a retailer near you, call toll-free 800-457-9112 or visit us at www.FoxChapelPublishing.com.

We are always looking for talented authors. To submit an idea, please send a brief inquiry to acquisitions@foxchapelpublishing.com.

Fox Chapel Publishing makes every effort to use environmentally friendly paper for printing.

Printed in China

WELCOME

CHAPTER ONE
FROM SWAMP TO
NATIONAL
PARK

Every year, about one million people explore Florida's Everglades National Park. Many come to see the wildlife, bringing cameras and binoculars to watch the hundreds of species of birds, fish, and reptiles. Others want to see the tangled knots of mangrove roots, the peeling bark of tourist trees, or the endless stretches of sawgrass. Still others go hiking, biking, or boating. Some take airboats or canoes through the Ten Thousand Islands area. At night, far from the lights of cities and towns, they can view a star-strewn sky.

Living in the Everglades

Today's Everglades started to form thousands of years ago in Orlando's Kissimmee River Basin, north of Lake Okeechobee. Over time, the water spread south, covering millions of acres of land. Different types of waterways were created, from shallow ponds to swampy sloughs. The wet season brought floods, and the dry season brought droughts. The changing water levels and temperatures created different ecosystems.

When humans tried to control the waterflow in Kissimmee River, plants and animals suffered. The Kissimmee River Restoration Project returned the river to its natural course.

The first people to live in the Everglades were Native American tribes, including the Calusa. For hundreds of years, small Calusa villages thrived in the southwestern parts of the swamp.[1] The Calusa spent their days fishing in the many waterways. They also hunted small game, such as turtles and alligators. The Calusa used turtle shells to make tools and jewelry. They also mixed the shells with clumps of dirt to build platforms, courtyards, and other shell works. Centuries later, these mounds of shells still stand.[2]

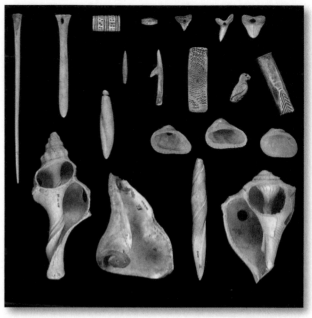

The Calusa used shells to make the tools they needed.

Other tribes lived in the Everglades, including the Tequesta, who settled in the east coast areas. They are known for building the Mud Lake Canal. Almost four miles long, this is one of the only prehistoric canoe canals left in North America. Historians

Mud Lake Canal is located near Flamingo, Florida.

believe the Tequesta used it for traveling between the Everglades and the Florida Keys.[3] The Calusa and Tequesta were severely impacted by

Native Americans hid in the mangrove forests during the Seminole wars in Florida.

disease brought by Spanish explorers. Native people who remained either fled deeper into the Everglades, or migrated to Cuba in the late 1700s.

As time passed, white settlers spread throughout the state of Florida. Several Native American tribes, including the Seminoles and Miccosukee, hid deep within the maze of the Everglades. Land ownership shifted from Britain to Spain, but by 1821, it finally belonged to the United States. Over the next few decades, the Seminole tribes and the United States fought, as President Jackson worked to remove all tribes from Florida through the Indian Removal Act. In 1856, the Seminoles signed a treaty, giving up two million acres of land to the United States.[4]

A New Century

As white settlers began moving into the area, they were not happy. It was full of strange plants, wild animals, and clouds of mosquitoes. How could they build homes and farms on this humid swampland?

The answer seemed simple: drain the extra water. By the 1880s, canals were being dug. Developers were making plans. The price of land skyrocketed.

While draining the swamp sounded simple, it was not. It took longer, cost more, and was less effective than anyone had thought.[5] Levees and dams changed the natural flow of water, threatening many species of animals and plants. As more people moved in, more canals, roads, and homes were built. Wildlife habitats were destroyed.

When landscape artist Ernest Coe visited the Everglades, he realized that this fragile ecosystem was in danger. He began the process of protecting the land. It took thirteen years of hard work, but finally, in 1947, the Everglades became a national park.

During the dedication ceremony, President Harry S. Truman told the country:

Each national park possesses qualities distinctive enough to make its preservation a matter of concern to the whole Nation. Certainly, this Everglades area has more than its share of features unique to these United States. Here are no lofty peaks seeking the sky, no mighty glaciers or rushing streams wearing away the uplifted land. Here is land, tranquil in its quiet beauty, serving not as the source of water but as the last receiver of it. To its natural abundance we owe the spectacular plant and animal life that distinguishes this place from all others in the country.[6]

PA-HAY-OKEE

Long before the Everglades became a national park, the land was known as *Pa-hay-okee,* or Grassy River. It was given this name by the Miccosukee people. This band of Seminoles moved to the Everglades after President Jackson chased them out of northern states. About 100 Miccosukee hid in the Everglades for more than one hundred years.

Many descendants of the original tribe still live there. They teach their children their traditions, language, and culture.

Every year in Florida, the Miccosukee people hold a festival to celebrate their traditions and culture.

CHAPTER TWO
HARDWOOD HAMMOCKS AND
PINE CANOPIES

As the water slowly wends its way through the Everglades, it dips and rises, speeding up and slowing down, creating sloughs, ponds, islands, and swamps. In one place, it stretches out farther than the eye can see, but it is only a few inches deep. Narrower channels and canals are up to three feet deep. The bottom is a thick layer of limestone, made from shells that have broken down and settled there. In some places, the water shimmers under the Florida sun, interrupted only by islands created by groves of trees. In others, the water peeks between clumps of sawgrass.

While most places in the U.S. have four seasons, the Everglades have only two: wet and dry. From December to April, the water slowly begins to recede. It is the dry season. Almost every day is sunny, with temperatures in the low to mid 80s. Less than two inches of rain falls each month. During these months, the risk of fire in the Everglades increases.

While most people think of fires as harmful, the ecosystem of the Everglades depends on them. Fires help

Ten Thousand Islands is where the Florida peninsula breaks up into thousands of little islands of mangrove clusters.

Sometimes fires are set on purpose in the northern Everglades. These controlled fires restore and maintain the ecosystem, reduce the threat of wildfires, stop pests and invasive species from spreading, and more.

certain plant and animal species to survive. In fact, if enough fires do not occur naturally, the fire management system for the Everglades will carefully start one. Controlled fires help the land in a number of ways. They reduce the leaves, branches, and other debris on the ground, they control the growth of certain plants, and maintain the habitats of many native species.[1]

From May to November, the wet season arrives. Temperatures are hot, in the mid to upper 90s. It rains and rains, and rains. Some months get as much as nine inches of rain! There have been years that have seen as much as 100 inches during this season.[2]

Each shift in the amount of water in the park creates a different type of landscape. Each one is unique and acts as home to the park's many species.

Sawgrass Marshes and Pine Forests

The Everglades has the largest sawgrass marshes in the world. This plant is considered a sedge. It looks like grass, but it is able to survive in water-soaked soil. During the wet season, the roots of the green, jagged sawgrass are completely under water. When a fire hits during the dry season, the dead clumps of sawgrass are burned away, and new plants grow in their place.

As the land in the Everglades gradually rises six to eight feet above the water line, pine forests grow. These are some of the highest spots in the park, so they are typically safe from flooding. The soil is sandy, and the

Sawgrass is not a true grass. Instead, it is a marsh-loving sedge.

Several types of pine trees grow in the pine forests, including slash pines. People used to "slash" these trees to harvest turpentine.

ground is rough and rocky, so water drains through it quickly. These areas depend on regular fires to thin out the growth and give the trees the room they need to grow well. Many of the pines have special bark that protects them from the heat of a fire.

Pine forests are home to more than trees and plants. They are also where you will find solution holes, which are natural pits in the ground. Small aquatic animals live in them when the holes fill with water. Long ago, alligators lived in some of these solution holes, but not enough water reaches the forests anymore to support such large animals. Many birds build nests on the branches of the trees around them. Air plants anchor themselves to the trunks and hang on tight.

Hardwood Hammocks and Mangrove Swamps

Sawgrass marshes are far too wet to support many trees. Just a few feet higher, however, hardwood trees, such as mahogany, gumbo-limbo, and cocoa palm, grow. These areas are known as hammocks. They are surrounded by a moat of water. Fallen leaves mix with rainwater and turn the water acidic. This dissolves the limestone bottom and creates the moat. These moats protect the hardwood trees from the fires that often sweep through the area.[3]

In the past, the hardwood hammocks were where Native Americans would build homes and plant crops. The thick canopy of leaves provided cooler temperatures, welcome shade from the sun, and protection from the mosquitoes. Today, visitors to the park can walk across a boardwalk so that they can see what it was like to live in such a lush, green place.

Boardwalks allow visitors to explore mangrove swamps without getting their feet wet.

A red mangrove.

Where the freshwater from Lake Okeechobee and the saltwater from the gulf and Florida Bay meet, they create a mix in which mangrove trees flourish but very little else will grow. These mangrove swamps cover more than 630 square miles within the national park. They are an essential part of protecting the coastlines. They also create new land by slowing the flow of water, allowing sediment to build up.[4] Some are white mangroves; others are red or black. All three types can tolerate high levels of salt, but the red can handle the most.

These trees produce seedlings, but the red mangrove has a special trick. The seeds sprout directly on the fruit of the tree. They do not fall off until late summer. The seedlings float in the water until they find enough land to take root. Soon another stand of mangrove trees is thriving.

The many different landforms found within the Everglades make it a very unusual place. They support a huge variety of animal and plant life. It is little wonder people come from all over the world to tour the park and witness the wonders of nature.

Marjory Stoneman Douglas, known as the "mother of the Everglades," once stated, "There are no other Everglades in the world. They are, they have always been, one of the unique regions of the earth; remote, never wholly known. Nothing anywhere else is like them."

ALL ABOARD THE GLADE SKIFFS

During the late nineteenth century, "gladesmen" moved through the Everglades in handmade glade skiffs. These boats were only two feet wide, but sixteen to eighteen feet long. They were designed to move easily through cramped waterways and canals.

The men stood at the back of the boat holding a long pole and used it to push their way through the mud and the shallowest water. After spending the day fishing, they would find a hammock on which to camp and hunt for food. They caught alligators, deer, turkey, rabbits, frogs, and turtles. What they did not eat, they sold.

As the rest of the world discovered the Everglades, the gladesmen acted as guides. The men knew the area so well that they could detect the slightest changes. As one expert wrote, "They were also able to interpret subtle signs in this landscape (such as slight depressions in the mud, the presence of certain birds, or specific odors) to track their prey."[5]

Glenn Simmons was a modern gladesman.

CHAPTER THREE
CREATURES OF THE
EVERGLADES

The blue heron stands so still in the marsh that it almost looks imagined. It has not moved in almost an hour. The bird is as tall as a young person, often reaching four feet or more. Everything about the bird is long: its S-shaped neck, its sharp beak, and its spindly legs. The heron stays perfectly still, waiting for a fish to forget it is there and swim just a little too close.

Suddenly, the heron's neck straightens out. The knife-like bill pierces the water and spears its dinner. In a single gulp, the bird swallows the fish whole. As it settles back into place to wait for another morsel to swim along, a second heron strolls through the water, watching for a snack. The two birds face each other. Who gets this territory? With a burst of feathers, the two flap their huge wings. They jump forward and back, then leap straight up into the air. They battle until one of the birds gives up and looks for another place to fish.[1]

The blue heron is the largest heron in North America.

Birds and Insects

Blue herons are one of 360 different species of birds found in the Everglades.[2] That may sound like a lot, but it is very few compared to a century ago, before humans changed the water flow. In the past, when groups of birds flew across the sky, huge shadows were cast on the ground. The famous naturalist and artist John James Audubon visited the Everglades in the 1800s. He wrote, "We observed great flocks of wading birds flying overhead toward their evening roosts...They appeared in such numbers to actually block out the light from the sun for some time."[3]

Wading birds, land birds, and birds of prey all make the Everglades their home. Some of them live there year-round. Others come during the winter months, and more stop by for just a few days or weeks on their way to a warmer or cooler climate.

The lesser yellowlegs are wading birds that spend the winter in the Everglades. They fly down from the northwest, as far as Alaska.

The white ibis is coral pink, just like the flamingo.

The Everglades is home to sixteen species of wading birds. Each has long, thin legs for walking and standing in the water while they wait for dinner to swim past. The white ibis has a curved beak for searching through the mud for the only food it likes: crayfish. Other waders include egrets, storks, flamingos, and the colorful roseate spoonbill.

The anhinga is a popular sight in the Everglades. Known as the snakebird, it has webbed feet and can swim. It sticks only its head and neck out of the water, so it looks like a snake gliding across the surface.[4]

The Cape Sable seaside sparrow is small, about five inches long, and has a yellow patch on the edge of each wing. The snail kite is unique

Osprey are large birds of prey. They are also known as fish hawks.

because it almost exclusively eats one thing: the apple snail.[5] The osprey is a bird of prey. When an osprey spots a fish in the water below, it dives straight down and snags it with its sharp talons.

Birds share the Everglades with many different kinds of insects. Whirligig beetles swim in fast circles, changing direction without any warning. They even dive under the water for a snack or take to the air for a quick flight.

A zebra longwing butterfly.

The Everglades hosts almost 100 species of butterflies, including the zebra longwing, the state's butterfly. The orange-and-black monarch is a common sight, sipping on nectar from flowering plants. Huge lubber grasshoppers jump from one leaf to another, while golden orb spiders spin webs from gold-colored silk. More dangerous eight-leggers include black widow spiders and scorpions. Centipedes and millipedes scurry across the ground on dozens to hundreds of legs. While millipedes eat dead and decaying plant matter, centipedes hunt other insects.[6]

Many Mammals

Forty species of mammals live throughout the Everglades. Bobcats dart in and out of the mangrove forests. Whitetail deer scamper through the sawgrass prairies. In the hardwood hammocks, gray squirrels scramble up and down tree trunks. The surprising marsh rabbit jumps in the water

Marsh rabbits have smaller ears and feet than wild mainland rabbits.

and swims. It has had to learn to do so, as it lives in a world of waterways.

Two mammals that live in the Everglades that are almost never spotted are the Florida panther and the black bear. There are fewer than 100 panthers left in the Everglades, as most were hunted to near extinction decades ago. They sleep during

Florida panther cubs.

A Florida black bear.

A Florida manatee.

the day, and hunt at dusk or dawn. The large Florida black bears were endangered for years, but they have been making a comeback.

Some of the Everglades' mammals live only in water, including the bottlenose dolphin and the endangered West Indian manatee. Manatees live in mangrove swamps. Slow swimmers, they are sometimes called sea cows.[7] They can be as long as thirteen feet and weigh up to 1,500 pounds. These large gray herbivores are distant relatives of elephants.

In the Water

Do you ever confuse alligators and crocodiles? Most people do, although they are two different creatures. Alligators live in freshwater, preferring the sloughs in the Everglades. They have rounded, U-shaped snouts. Males grow to about eleven feet long. Crocodiles, on the other hand, prefer saltwater, so they are at home in the mangrove forests. They have long, V-shaped snouts. Males

Alligators can be found in any body of freshwater in Florida.

can grow as long as twenty feet. The Everglades is the only place in the world where both of these reptiles are found in the wild.

Other reptiles share this habitat: boa constrictors, water snakes, and king snakes slither around. Sixteen types of turtles and tortoises live in the park, from the common striped mud turtle to the rarely seen stinkpot and Atlantic Leatherback. The tiniest frog in North America, the Little Grass frog, also lives there. It is as small as a person's fingernail.

Unwelcome Species

There are hundreds of wildlife species in the Everglades, but not all of them are welcome. These uninvited guests are called invasive species. They are not natural to the area, but have been brought in accidentally by visitors or by the pet and plant markets. These species often thrive in the Everglades, but they cause serious problems for the native plants

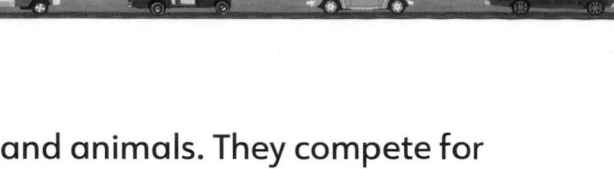

A lionfish.

and animals. They compete for food, and since many of them have no natural predators, they can reproduce quickly. Often, the invaders conquer the native species, and this can leave gaping holes in the food web.[8]

Two of these invasive creatures are the lionfish and Burmese python. The lionfish is a poisonous fish brought to this part of the world in the 1980s. In the Everglades, the lionfish consume so much food that other species starve.

Thousands of Burmese pythons are living in the Everglades. Most of them are descendants of released or escaped pet snakes. As one of

the largest snake species in the world, these pythons are spreading quickly. They are hunting larger and larger native animals. Although 2,000 pythons were removed from the Everglades between 2002 and 2013, experts believe that this number is only a tiny fraction of the pythons that remain in the park.[9]

A Burmese python.

THE FATHER OF THE EVERGLADES

Ernest F. Coe

Ernest F. Coe (1866–1951) might have been known as Tom to his friends, but to the rest of the country, he became known as "the father of the Everglades." Born in Connecticut, he and his wife, Anna, moved to Miami in 1925.

Coe loved spending his days outside, and it was not long before he came across the Everglades. As much as he loved the beautiful land, he was equally worried about the way the wildlife was being destroyed. When his wife told him the only way to stop the destruction was to turn the region into a national park, Coe had a new goal.[10]

According to Michael Grunwald, author of a book about Coe, he explored every inch of the Everglades. "Sixty years old and unemployed, with no outlet for his boundless energy, he began sloshing around the Everglades in canvas sneakers, often wrapping himself in a blanket and sleeping in the middle of the marsh," he wrote. "Coe fell madly in love with this 'great empire of solitude.'"[11]

Coe drew up maps, wrote thousands of letters, headed committees, and established the Tropical Everglades National Park Association in 1928. It was because of his passion and hard work that the Everglades became a national park. The park's visitor center is named after Coe to honor his dedication.

CHAPTER FOUR
TREES ON STILTS AND PLANTS
LIVING ON AIR

What do most trees need to survive? A steady supply of freshwater is often the first element. Not so with the mangroves! They grow best on a constantly changing supply of brackish water, which is a mix of freshwater and saltwater. The roots soak up the salt and store it in the trees' leaves. Later, it sheds its leaves, clearing out the salt.

Trees also need sturdy underground roots to anchor them and to draw up nutrients. Once again, the bizarre mangrove trees are just the opposite. Their roots grow *above* the soil, making it look as if they are on stilts. These tangled roots keep the trunks and leaves above the water, even during high tide.[1]

The mangroves are not just unusual—they are also extremely important to the ecosystem of the Everglades. The root systems reach down into the mud, providing a place for fish and other creatures to hide from predators and search for food. They protect the park's coastlines

The red mangrove is the most common type of mangrove in Florida.

and prevent the edges from eroding. Their roots slow down the flow of brackish water. Sediments sift down through the water to create a thick, rich, muddy bottom. This layer helps make the coastline stronger, protecting it from strong winds, powerful waves, and storm surges.[2]

Mangroves are only one of the many incredible trees growing in the Everglades. A combination of warmth, water, and protection from people has left this national park extremely rich in plant life. In fact, about 750 different kinds of native seed-bearing plants are spread across its acres.

Tremendous Trees

Besides mangroves, the park includes bald cypress, slash pine, gumbo-limbo, royal palm, and strangler fig. The bald cypress is one of the many types of cypress trees in the area. It drops its leaves during the dry season, making it look bald. The base, or buttress, of the tree is as large as six feet across. It helps secure the tree in the shallow soil. One of the most unusual features of these trees is the "knees" that grow on their roots. These knees poke out of the ground, and experts believe they are used for breathing.[3]

An egret hunts among the roots of bald cypress trees.

The slash pine has layers of bark and produces cones, like many pine trees. These cones hold very thin seeds—food for birds, squirrels, and other mammals. The tree's sap has been used in making sealants, turpentine, paint thinners, antiseptics, and more.

The gumbo-limbo tree is sometimes called the "tourist tree" because it has bright red bark that peels, just like a tourist with sunburn.[4] If strong winds knock it over, it can grow back from little more than a broken branch.

The royal palm is so common in the park that it has an area named for it. It

A gumbo-limbo tree.

often soars as high as eighty feet into the air, and its gray trunk looks like a column of cement.[5]

The strangler fig earns its name for a good reason. The seeds of this tree are usually carried by birds and dropped into a crack in another type of tree. The seeds sprout and long, thin roots wind down the tree to the ground below. As the fig grows, it begins to strangle the tree it is growing on, eventually killing it and taking its place in the Everglades.[6]

Strangler figs take root near the base of the host tree.

Plentiful Plants and Flowers

Looking across a marsh full of sawgrass reminds visitors how the park earned the nickname "River of Grass." Sawgrass spreads out in all directions, rippling in the wind like waves. It can grow to be nine feet high. With thick stems that grow deep underground, the grass provides the perfect hiding place—or snack—for animals.[7] Sawgrass leaves look like saw blades. They are so sharp, they can cut bare skin, similar to a paper cut.

Sawgrass is one of more than 100 different marsh species growing in the Everglades. Other marsh species include bladderwort, spatterdock, and maidencane. Bladderwort's name is based on the small bladders, or sacs it carries on its leaves. The bladders capture and digest periphyton algae. Other creatures also dine on these tiny organisms, including snails and crayfish, minnows, and certain types of ducks and turtles.

Another fascinating type of plant found in the Everglades is the air plant. Unlike plants that need soil to grow, air plants—also known as epiphytes—root themselves to other plants. They get the nutrients they need from the air around them. These include Spanish moss, green ferns, and wild orchids. The largest orchid is the cowhorn, which can weigh as much as seventy-five pounds!

More than twenty types of ferns are also found in the park, including the resurrection fern, or "the poor man's barometer." When the weather is dry, the leaves curl up and turn brown. When the leaves unfold and turn bright green, rain is on its way.

Pink air plants are related to pineapples. Their leaves absorb food and water, so they do not need soil to grow.

THE MOTHER OF THE EVERGLADES

Marjory Stoneman Douglas

Many people refer to the Everglades as the "River of Grass." The name was made popular by Marjory Stoneman Douglas (1890–1998), sometimes called the "mother of the Everglades."[8]

But it was not love at first sight when Douglas visited the Everglades. In fact, she labeled it "too buggy, too wet, too generally inhospitable." Nonetheless, she agreed to work with conservationist Ernest Coe, and saving this special land became her main mission. In 1947, she published *The Everglades: River of Grass* to raise people's awareness of the region. In it, she brought the land to life for readers. She wrote, "The miracle of the light pours over the green and brown expanse of sawgrass and of water, shining and slow-moving below, the grass and water that is the meaning and the central fact of the Everglades of Florida."[9]

Douglas spent her life helping to protect the Everglades. In 1986, an award was named in her honor. It was given to those who dedicate their lives to helping national parks. In 1993, she was given the Presidential Medal of Freedom. She passed away five years later at the age of 108. Not surprisingly, her ashes were scattered in the Everglades.

CHAPTER FIVE
FACING A FRIGHTENING
FUTURE

As much as Everglades National Park is treasured, it is also in trouble. Ever since the first settlers drained the land and altered the water flow by building dikes and dams, the land has been paying a heavy price.

While the Everglades cover millions of acres, it is half the size it was just a century ago.[1] Before it was declared a park, a lot of the land was used for homes and farms. State flood control projects also interfered with the natural flow of water. To reduce the risk of annual floods, canals and levees were built. These projects saved thousands of acres of farmland from flooding, but they also left former wetlands dry as a bone. Two new highways divided the Everglades into smaller parts and further altered the water flow.[2]

Each change sparked a domino effect. The diet and habitat of plants and animals changed, creating challenges that many species could not overcome. For example, environmental changes caused the number of

The main purpose of levees is to prevent flooding.

35

wading birds in the Everglades to drop by ninety percent.[3] Animals, such as the Florida panther, were nearly wiped out. Experts believe there are only about 100 of the panthers left in the Everglades.

The Problem of Pollution

Perhaps one of the biggest dangers facing the Everglades today is water pollution. During the late 1980s, experts found a great deal of phosphorus in much of the water inside the park. Most of it came as runoff from sugarcane plantations. These plantations relied heavily on fertilizers containing phosphorus. Phosphorus encouraged the growth of specific types of plant life, including cattails. Although cattails are native to the Everglades, they grew out of control. They pushed out other native plants. Animals that depended on those plants suffered as well.

Sugarcane is a main crop in Florida. Farmers use fertilizers to help it grow. The fertilizer often runs off the farmland and into rivers and streams, changing the habitat for plants and animals.

Stormwater Treatment Areas are used to remove phosphorus from water before it is allowed to flow into the Everglades.

   In 1988, the federal government sued the state of Florida over the phosphorus. The state worked to reduce the contamination by creating Stormwater Treatment Areas. These artificial marshes would filter and clean water before it entered the Everglades. It often took months, but it was effective. The amount of phosphorus dropped from 150 parts per billion to ten parts per billion.[4]

   Phosphorus is not the only pollutant in the Everglades' water. Fish caught in the area showed high levels of mercury. In fact, they showed some of the highest levels ever found in the country! But where does the mercury come from? Some people believe much of it comes from the same sugarcane plantations in the form of sulfur.[5] The sulfur mixes with the natural mercury in the water, creating the poison methyl mercury.

Other scientists think that the mercury found in the water actually comes from thousands of miles away. Scientists believe it travels on trade winds and enters the Everglades through rain. In an interview with CNN, Tom Atkeson, mercury coordinator of the Florida Department of Environmental Protection, stated, "Of the mercury getting into the Everglades each year, at least ninety-five percent of it is coming out of the air." The argument over who really is at fault—and who should pay for repairing the damage—continues in Florida.[6]

The Goals of CERP

How can people continue to protect the Everglades? One step was taken in 2000 with CERP, the Comprehensive Everglades Restoration Plan. The main goal of CERP is to restore, protect, and preserve the ecosystem of the Everglades.[7]

Its goals are immense and expensive. As of June 2022, the cost of the plan was an estimated $23.2 billion, and could take until 2050 to complete. The number one purpose of CERP is to capture the billions of gallons of freshwater now flowing into the ocean and redirect it to the areas in the Everglades that need it the most.[8] In addition, more than 240 miles of canals and levees would be removed to restore the original flow of the water.

As President Truman reminded the nation more than sixty years ago, "Today we mark the achievement of another great conservation victory. We have permanently safeguarded an irreplaceable primitive area. We have assembled to dedicate the use of all people for all time, the Everglades National Park."[9]

That "irreplaceable primitive area" may need some help to keep surviving, and thriving, so that generations to come can appreciate this national park "for all time."

VISITING THE RIVER OF GRASS

Everglades National Park is open every day of the year, twenty-four hours a day, although some entrances are closed at sunset hours. There are four visitor centers on the grounds. They feature a wide variety of wares, from insect repellant to paintings by local artists.

All visitors are given a special warning: Look out for vultures! Black vultures are native to the park. For some reason, these birds are attracted to the black rubber and vinyl parts found on windshields, windshield wipers, and sunroofs. To protect their cars, visitors are encouraged to cover any exposed rubber pieces with plastic tarps, wet towels, or paper. It's a vulture alert![10]

Cover your car or black vultures might swipe your windshield wipers!

FUN FACTS

- Everglades National Park covers 1.5 million acres.
- One out of every three people living in Florida depends on the Everglades for their water supply.[1]
- The Everglades is home to sixty-seven threatened or endangered species.
- Twenty-six percent of the mammals, birds, reptiles, amphibians, and fish in the Everglades are not native to the region.[2]
- The Everglades is the only place on the entire planet to find the American crocodile and the American alligator coexisting in the wild.
- The Everglades contains more than 200 known archeological sites.
- The official birthday for Everglades National Park is December 6.
- The Everglades is listed as a Ramsar Wetland of International Importance, a World Heritage Site, and an International Biosphere Reserve.
- Everglades National Park is very close to Cuba. During the 1950s, the park was used for a number of Cold War operations. It was also used as a training center for CIA agents, a shooting range, an air defense site, and a weapons lab.

Chapter 1

1. "Everglades National Park Florida." National Park Service.
2. "National Park System Areas Listed in Chronological Order of Date Authorized Under DOI." National Park Service.
3. "Native People." National Park Service: Everglades. http://www.nps.gov/ever/historyculture/native-people.htm
4. "Miccosukee Tribe of Indiana of Florida." Miccosukee Tribe of Indians of Florida.
5. Landry, Clay J. "Who Drained the Everglades?" *PERC*, Spring 2002, http://perc.org/articles/who-drained-the-everglades
6. Harry Truman. "231—Address on Conservation at the Dedication of Everglades National Park." *The American Presidency Project.*

Chapter 2

1. "An Ecosystem Management Tool." National Park Service: Everglades. http://www.nps.gov/ever/parkmgmt/ecosystemmanagement.htm
2. The Weather Channel. "Monthly Averages for Everglades National Park." http://www.weather.com/weather/wxclimatology/monthly/graph/USFL0138
3. "Everglades National Park." Park Vision.
4. Ibid.
5. "Gladesmen." National Park Service: Everglades. http://www.nps.gov/ever/historyculture/gladesmen.htm

Chapter 3

1. "Great Blue Heron." *National Geographic.* http://animals.nationalgeographic.com/animals/birds/great-blue-heron/
2. "Birds." National Park Service: Everglades. http://www.nps.gov/ever/naturescience/birds.htm
3. Ibid.
4. "Anhinga." *Nature Works.* http://www.nhptv.org/natureworks/anhinga.htm
5. "Plants and Animals of the Everglades." *The Journey to Restore America's Everglades.*
6. "Insects, Spiders, Centipedes, Millipedes." National Park Service: Everglades. http://www.nps.gov/ever/naturescience/insects.htm
7. "West Indian Manatee: Species Profile." National Park Service: Everglades. http://www.nps.gov/ever/naturescience/manateepage.htm
8. "Invasive Animal Program." National Park Service: Everglades. http://www.nps.gov/ever/naturescience/invasiveanimalprogram.htm
9. "Burmese Pythons." National Park Service: Everglades.
10. Chris Woodside. "Father of the Everglades." *Connecticut Woodlands,* Fall 2012.
11. Ibid.

Chapter 4

1. "What Is a 'Mangrove' Forest?" National Ocean Service. http://oceanservice.noaa.gov/facts/mangroves.html
2. Ibid.
3. "So You Want to Know More about . . . Plants and Animals of the Everglades." *The Journey to Restore America's Everglades.*
4. Susana Cortazar. "A Tree Peels at Zoo Miami—the Gumbo Limbo Tree, aka 'The Tourist Tree.' " Miami Zoo.
5. "So You Want to Know More about . . . Plants and Animals of the Everglades."
6. "Everglades National Park: Plant Life." GORP.
7. "Trees and Plants of the Florida Everglades." Garden Guides. http://www.gardenguides.com/95744-trees-plants-florida-everglades.html
8. PBS. "Marjory Stoneman Douglas (1890–1998)." *The National Parks: America's Best Idea.* http://www.pbs.org/nationalparks/people/behindtheparks/douglas/
9. Ibid.

Chapter 5

1. "Florida Everglades." Natural Resources Defense Council. http://www.nrdc.org/water/conservation/qever.asp#threats
2. William H. Orem. " Pollutants Threaten the Everglades' Future." *Earth.* February 20, 2009.
3. "Florida Everglades."
4. Orem.
5. John Zarrella. "Study: Mercury in Everglades Comes from Distant Sources." CNN.com. February 13, 1998. http://www.cnn.com/EARTH/9802/13/everglades.mercury/
6. "FAQ: Everglades Toxic Mercury Levels Threaten Human Health and Wildlife." Friends of the Everglades.
7. "FAQs: What You Should Know About the Comprehensive Everglades Restoration Plan (CERP)." *The Journey to Restore America's Everglades.*
8. "About CERP: Brief Overview." *The Journey to Restore America's Everglades.*
9. "Quotes." National Park Service: Everglades. http://www.nps.gov/ever/parknews/quotes.htm
10. "Visitors and Vultures: What to Know." National Park Service: Everglades. http://www.nps.gov/ever/planyourvisit/vulturestoknow.htm

Fun Facts

1. "Cold War in South Florida: Historic Resource Study." National Park Service, p. 39.
2. "Top 10 Scariest Facts about the Everglades." *Environment Florida,* October 31, 2011, http://www.environmentflorida.org/news/fle/top-10-scariest-facts-about-everglades

Works Consulted

Ali Childs, Arcynta. "Attack of the Giant Pythons." *Smithsonian*, April 2011.

"Anhinga." *Nature Works.* http://www.nhptv.org/natureworks/anhinga.htm

"Cold War in South Florida: Historic Resource Study." National Park Service.

Cortazar, Susana. "A Tree Peels at Zoo Miami—the Gumbo Limbo Tree, aka 'The Tourist Tree.'" Miami Zoo.

"Everglades National Park." http://www.shannontech.com/ParkVision/Everglades/Everglades.html#EvergladesLandforms

"Everglades National Park." GORP.

"Florida: The Everglades." The Nature Conservancy. http://www.nature.org/ourinitiatives/regions/northamerica/unitedstates/florida/placesweprotect/everglades.xml

Goudarzi, Sara. "Scientists Finally Figure Out How Bees Fly." *Live Science.* January 9, 2006. http://www.livescience.com/528-scientists-finally-figure-bees-fly.html

"Great Blue Heron." *National Geographic.* http://animals.nationalgeographic.com/animals/birds/great-blue-heron/

Journey to Restore America's Everglades, The.

Landry, Clay J. "Who Drained the Everglades?" *PERC,* Spring 2002. http://perc.org/articles/who-drained-the-everglades

"Mangrove Forests." Blue Planet Biomes.org. http://www.blueplanetbiomes.org/mangrove_forests.htm

National Park Service: Everglades. http://www.nps.gov/ever/index.htm

"National Park System Areas Listed in Chronological Order of Date Authorized Under DOI." National Park Service.

Orem, William H. " Pollutants Threaten the Everglades' Future." *Earth.* February 20, 2009.

Park, Paula. "A Brief History of the Miccosukees." *Miami New Times,* December 12, 1996.

PBS. *The National Parks: America's Best Idea.* http://www.pbs.org/nationalparks/people/behindtheparks/douglas/

Toops, Connie. *The Florida Everglades.* Minneapolis: Voyageur Press, 1998.

"Top 10 Scariest Facts about the Everglades." *Environment Florida,* October 31, 2011. http://www.environmentflorida.org/news/fle/top-10-scariest-facts-about-everglades

Truman, Harry. "231—Address on Conservation at the Dedication of Everglades National Park." The American Presidency Project.

Truman Library Photographs, Harry S. Truman Library and Museum,

Weather Channel, The. "Monthly Averages for Everglades National Park." http://www.weather.com/weather/wxclimatology/monthly/graph/USFL0138

"What Is a 'Mangrove' Forest?" National Ocean Service. http://oceanservice.noaa.gov/facts/mangroves.html

Woodside, Chris. "Father of the Everglades." *Connecticut Woodlands,* Fall 2012.

Zarrella, John. "Study: Mercury in Everglades Comes from Distant Sources." *CNN.com,* February 13, 1998. http://www.cnn.com/EARTH/9802/13/everglades.mercury/

Further Reading

Benoit, Peter. *Wetlands.* New York: Scholastic, 2011.

Frisch, Max. *Preserving America: Everglades National Park.* Mankato, MN: Creative Press, 2014.

Lasky, Kathryn. *John Muir: America's First Environmentalist.* Somerville, MA: Candlewick Press, 2014.

McCarthy, Pat. *Friends of the Earth: A History of American Environmentalism with 21 Activities.* Chicago: Chicago Review Press, 2013.

Rappaport, Doreen. *To Dare Mighty Things: The Life of Theodore Roosevelt.* New York: Disney-Hyperion, 2013.

Websites

Everglades National Park for Kids
   http://www.nps.gov/ever/forkids/index.htm

Florida Department of Environmental Protection Kid's Page
   http://floridadep.gov/kidzone

barometer (buh-RAH-muh-ter)—A weather instrument is used to determine air pressure, which predicts the chance of rain.

brackish (BRAK-ish)—Slightly salty; having a mixture of saltwater in freshwater.

buttress (BUH-tress)—A support or base.

ecosystem (EE-koh-sis-tem; EH-koh-sis-tem)—A biological community of living creatures and their environment.

epiphyte (EH-pee-fyt)—Any plant that usually grows on another plant and gets moisture and nutrients from the air and rain.

eroding (ee-ROH-ding)—Gradual wearing away of soil, rock, or land by wind or water.

levee (LEH-vee)—A wall built to keep a river from overflowing.

periphyton algae (payr-ee-FY-ton AL-jee)—Tiny freshwater organisms attached to or clinging to plants and rocks.

phosphorus (FOS-for-us)—A chemical used in fertilizers.

restoration (res-tor-AY-shun)—The process of putting something back the way it was.

runoff (RUN-off)—The draining away of water from the surface of an area of land.